blinking with fists

BILLY CORGAN

•

BILLY CORGAN is the singer and songwriter for the critically acclaimed, multiplatinum Chicago band The Smashing Pumpkins. He is at work on his first novel.

T0057932

blinking with fists

FARRAR, STRAUS AND GIROUX

NEW YORK

•

blinking
with fists

BILLY CORGAN

Farrar, Strauss & Giroux
18 West 18th Street, New York 10011

First paperback edition, 2006

The Library of Congress has cataloged the hardcover
edition as follows:
Corgan, Billy.
    Blinking with fists / Billy Corgan.— 1st ed.
       p.   cm.
    ISBN-13: 978-0-571-21189-0
    ISBN-10: 0-571-21189-5 (alk. paper)
    I. Title.

PS3603.O7344B55 2004
813'.6—dc22

                                    2004047100

Paperback ISBN-13: 978-0-571-21170-8
Paperback ISBN-10: 0-571-21170-4

Designed by Gretchen Achilles
Title page art by Yelena Yemchuk

www.fsgbooks.com

P1

This book is dedicated to my mother,
Martha Louise Maes Corgan Lutz

I would like to extend my eternal gratitude to those souls who have touched my heart, of whom for me there have been many. I have known many teachers along the way, and few loves, but all of them are here with me. All credit is placed in the arms of God, who thought this whole deal up. God blesses me every day with the greatest of wonders, and points me well into light and shadow alike. I can't say I mind too much.

BILLY CORGAN
Chicago, March 12, 2004

contents

blinking with fists

the poetry of my heart

Revealing now the poetry of my heart
Think birds in flight and you will start to come close
As faces come from the darkness familiar
To greet you hello again
They pluck those strings and sing those refrains I know so well, and
    hold so close
Now follow these birds faithfully, keeping those faces in mind
Over rivers and dales and soft greens until we come to the edge of
    the vast ocean
The biggest sea you may imagine and more
Lift your hand and let those birds soar with this sweet music

Fast we fly over these waters
Faster and faster until we blur, and our words blur, and memories
    of lost things blur too
The sun catches you flying
Imagine this from the perspective of the sun
Those birds and you moving the speed of light over the blue
Well, if you were the sun, you'd laugh too!
Finally, after such a momentous journey
You slow upon a deserted island, lush with life
And on its barren shore you find a worn sea chest
Polished smooth by years of coarse handling
Open that chest and you would find inside
A single valentine and the poetry of my heart
Dragging that sea chest around the bend
Thru sand into a jungle dense with flower and shade
We take the forgotten trail up the hillside
Up towards the laughing sun

Catching its wisdom as it's given
Past the ghost whispers and relics of another past
Climbing to the very top
Because time will not stand still for us
But it will pretend every once in a while
And up here, forgotten, is just you, me
One sea chest holding a single valentine and the poetry of our
    hearts

A single bulb lights this room
It's dark in here all the time
If the ceiling had only captured my dreams and nightmares alike,
    what stories it could show
She is here, the one
The one I love, desire, devise, rescue, all to my heart's own sorrow
I'm lost in this room, but this is the place the valentines are written
The site of my greatest thought and saddest song
There are no birds here to take flight
No oceans to fly over, no islands to reach
No sun to catch me crying
This is the gift of oblivion and opaque dance

Revealing now the poetry of my own heart
Its sorrow and the nameless wish I called bliss once
Stripped of its title and junked for show
The bulbs swing, the kids sing
The rooster crows and I seek sleep
Somewhere past the scars and empty cars and endless bars filled
    with reminders

I want to climb from this hole
And dash myself upon the rocks below
But still it requires your push
Because a push requires intent
And intent requires desire
And desire registers in this body as need
Do you need me?
So push me over, my sea chest and me
The birds will follow me down

Retrace the steps, up to the ceiling
Back thru the bulb, into the electric wires
And out of Manhattan
Coming out another side
To a kid, a dream
A scrawled valentine with an x and o if truth be told
Revealing now the poetry of my heart
Rage and the canopies it paints
And the drawings it frames
And its real cage, me

half-light, half-life

My senses open to this time and place
Stutter steps and craning necks and we all fall about the place
This is where we came to hold hands
To wait on promises made good
By tradition and sorrows
My voice came, and the planes came
And they opened up their bays to the blue sky crying for some rain
And rain they did
And took my place
And made a little check mark next to my heart
To remember this place for some other day

To live in half-life is exactly as it sounds
Half-taste, half-pain, half-dead
But wide awake
In half-light
I figure now I've lived just 18 years
As the other half of me, in mothballs and vanilla crème
Patiently holds out for a little more than fallen bells tumbling
Her crosses bent like me
As we wave, the family and I, to what was
What was lives in the shadows
But it is the shadow of God's grace
My shadows all man-made gray and smoky turns
Come along to this place where we stood
Proud and happy and so, understood
Thus faith will follow faith
And love should follow love

look

Look
How beautiful the trees
Draw a circle around
Such simple theater is pleasing
If you say "stay"
Here and now
And once in the again
Faces painted and children at the ready
Draw your swords
We're off, we're off
How beautiful are we

This autumn, more bronzed than the last
Cemented us here
Chained to the oracle's missives of woe
Her breath sweet with futures sewn
Carving horses into elephant bones
Be safe, when you go

My glasses misplaced
I seem to have lost my page
Oh yes, where was I?
Tiptoeing thru graves
I find no sleep in this grotto
That is no mistake
I know you can't be erased
But I can try

Whoever now holds the infinite wisdoms of the secret universe
  (for me)
Thank you (for that)
Cause I often forget
What used to so easily come to mind
And those stories should be kept safe

in the wake of poseidon

She held the pearl to her lips
Pushing it between her little teeth to shine
In waters crystal clear and reflective
I caused a certain dancing around the eyes
Spellbound! I was cast in an unlikely role
Seafarer, captain of the ship
I cut the lines to shore and said her prayer of honor
Did I mention the pearl was gray?
So in the wake of Poseidon did we reach and stretch
Up and out and towards
Dancing beneath all stars to behold
Now these are lazy scenes to paint
But it's the breeze, the soft warm summer breeze
That I most wish to convey
A tempest without sound
Sneaking up on us in seagull cries
And her burbles and gurgles from down below
So out there we were all alone
In the wake
Drifting to and further fro
Caught between delight and what you know

lost gray

Gray spot lost
The birds they spy
For gods
Watch!
From the cracks in bell towers we watch
Leaning
Laughing like lost souls
My mind says shhhh!
Peace is come
Pick a spot to swing down upon

Stir, the crow cackle
Collar high
The angles black against the sides
Splitting in 2's we swing clubs
Old fog rolls and hugs
Back slappin'
Paying dues for crackjaws

Jimmyknives whistle
The steam train turns
Into pipes thick with vermin slick
Take your pick
Me or him
Be quick and fix
Flesh is waxen
Thighs high
Saxon deeds
Curry the eye

Now run, fast as you're done
Spineneedle whither
Winter she numbs
Sound the signal
Together we wire
Ride juiced umbrellas
Into the spires

From cracks in bell towers
We lean into days
Laughing like lost souls unafraid
My ears say stop!
You mustn't move
Peace is here

the sun of flowers

The way
You look
At me
Makes me
Lonely
Grinding tears
Behind a mask
Made of
Abalone
Counting fingers
Inside
My fist
Spitting amethyst
Into pits
Dug for fire
Uncovered
I am dancing
They are coming
My sacrifice
Laughing
Flailing wrists
Powerless
The season at hand
Anointing this
Forgive
Forget
No witness
A myth
Of clover kissed

Deathwish

Moss grows

Over my body

You watch

The sun of flowers

Move quick

Dig a trench

Get in

Head down

Wait

No escape

Action

They're coming in

4 leaf clover kissed

Forgiveness

I miss forgiveness

Cleaving me

Leaving me

Restless

Pillows of moss

Watching sheep

Jump the horse

To bed they rise

The way

You look

Makes me

Lonely

Forgive

Forget

The sun of hours
Goes round
The knife
Their sacrifice
Outside
Time
Blood rites
Drinking hyacinth
Carcass
Opal shores
To the sea
I believe
I will sink
Deeper than deep
Forgive
Forget me
Lonely sea
The sun of flowers is coming

li-lo, li-lo

The indecision speaks volumes for all to hear
I clear all paths before me
Thinking in time, without a worrying mind
That I will come to a place of rest
A last caress, perhaps of chance
My hand on your belly, I softly begin to sing
Li-lo, li-lo, li-lo
Pulling from you what little I need
Freeze the moment, make it last
What you have can never rush past

I comply in silence for fear and no trust
To soak the vinegar from your lips
To taste the spy in your kiss
Set me loose upon you all, show me how
I dare not speak, I'm weak, too weak
But my reign shall wreak such terrors upon
Wherever there is
Is pause for alarm

You swore you met a different man
Not the one who bends before you now
You swore you'd love a different sort
Than I who swear all before you

Embrace, forsake, go ahead it makes you
The mistakes don't stop, let it chase you

I taste, relate, to invade you
No wait, I'll change, and await you
So cry no tears of missing out
Cry for those who go without

barbarians

Muted tones and half-tones
Barbarians watch me quiet like
"it's important that you arrive at such and such a place at such and
        such a date"
okay, I think I understand
rebellion is a chore
under these circumstances misguided
pointless
must save energy
turn insights into action
buck up
deliver on a scale of new dimensions
expand the box
kill the feeling
systems on, check
communications poor
white sand in my hair, in my mouth
it pours out as I speak
I can't be rid of its reminder
Uncovering
Skeleton key
Boxes in the basement
Debris from past unions
Hastily packed
Make a new hiding place
Ring the bell
Now sleep
Now wish

Now arise
Now eat
Now move
Now survey what's left

on the maypole

around the maypole with childish eye
rushing thru autumn days
wrapping blankets around frames
wishing in the sky
no matter where you stand
you stand here with me
missing simple times
mixing blood with rose oil
we are leaving too soon
to make new friends
we shall not remember

a twixt the twine

A twixt the twine and flowers divine
Devise the deign in this copper wane
Aghast the mask of ripping change
Aloft amongst the highest paid

Blend in the softer hues
Bespeak of melon and her honey fuse
Light my ire's with playful trust
For devour you insatiable I must
So mixed the mire the many did soar
Sour the supine on slippery floor
Green the grievous wound poured into salt
Salacious and sated the savory sport

Don't get certain, play tricks with mine pull
Gather your colours and ever your sulk
No manners in me matter the most
Than playing valour to your consummate host
Pillow the phenom on purring divan
Mellow the missing on vanilla white toast
Laboured amongst the living lull last
Repay the repast in revolting rake

Never come give it up
Whatever you may squander
The figs in pocket and the cousins down under
By blood are the passions passing us up
By pill is the poison feeling
The heat it kills me every day

By graveyard vigil and candles I bake
Kitchens are aching for archangel falls
Of soft baby bottoms and polished skulls
Amen!

A twixt the twine and flowers divine
Devise the deign in this copper wane
Aghast the mask of ripping change
As I lie, aloft amongst the highest paid

artificial love poem

To fill this page
To write this rage
To pull this moment square

I am not nature
or dust
but I am made of such

I stood waiting for you to run
In sweet-smelling lilac I stood
waiting for you to dance

Holding our breath in brackish water until one of us should die
I took the chance because we used to laugh
Oh how we used to laugh!

How greed fills my cup
with betrayal of all that is dust
And all that ever was

blinking with fists (and other caterpillar tales)

A poem, if you will:
Gentle waves rise
Just off the fingertips
All I breathe is mine
By name alone
Shape-shifter questions
To strip skin off slow
Devoid of sex
I mix up unions in the offering
The hushed-up voices are here
But they are sated full
Waiting for the stumble
That must surely come
"this time," he declares loudly
(anonymous town square)
"this time there will be no stumble"
and the crowd, on cue, erupts wildly in unison, "hooray"

while I sleep they come in pairs
to pat my head and teach old verse
I try to tell them my life is redundant
By placing my finger to my temple to show knowing
With bruises at the ready I am
Blinking with fists

The chorus lines up to sing
A deep breath, ready to begin

A crying baby breaks the silence
Awkward laughter ensues, on cue
"divine order," says someone

falling down chimneys, thru veins, out limbs
into masterpieces drawn in dirt
the figures are portrayed in a stunning act of repose
their bindings on their wrists
they are still blinking

the others

If the dream is gone
Good!, then let it die
I'd rather tumble from my window
To ground wet and hard with rain
Knowing you were waiting for me
Hearing the gravel scrape under our feet
Counting long seconds between cars passing
To cross the road giddy with freedom
There is something about your face
Lit up by the station lights
That inspires me to reach out past you
and this moment
And try to take you with me
I know you won't come
this town has already killed you
and it's my desire in your eyes
I will echo your print forward
And attempt to copy you numerous ways in the coming years
But I don't know all that now
When the watchers die
They will try to take us with them
To keep them company, repeat the story line
I miss you already
Starting for home
The zombies keeping
All of it for themselves
Lest another one of us comes
And tries to leave with their share

Good night angels
Good night sky
Tomorrow I take leave

chiaroscuro

Paint your face with ashes
(Paint your face in ashes)
Draw your face in coal
(Draw your face with coal)
A woman without son
(A woman without son)
Is a man without soul
(A man missing soul)

The train leaves at 4
(The train departs at four)
Please don't be late
(Please, don't be late)
Don't forget your paper
(Don't forget the papers)
Give a kiss when you leave
(kiss me when you disappear)

The man he whispers when the moon is low
(The man he whispers when the tide is low)
Naked desire waiting to be told
(Naked desire, waiting to be told)
There's pity in his heart for every living thing
(There's a pity in his heart for every living thing)
In the blood of a thousand dreams
(In his blood, a thousand dreams)

He bought himself a ticket to the end of the line
(He bought himself a ticket to the end of the line)

He rode quietly, reading his mind
(He rode quiet, erasing time)
Loneliness found him, and found a seat next to him
(Loneliness came and sat next to him)
Together they rode silently, observing the shift
(They rode together in silence, listening to the wind)

He found a trident by the sea
(By the sea a trident he did find)
What he saw you won't believe
(What he saw you cannot believe)
He witnessed power, then shadow, then he saw me
(He saw power and shadow, and witnessed me)
We prayed for peace in every living thing
(We prayed for peace for every living thing)

The scourge of Apollo hovers everywhere
(The filth of Apollo is everywhere)
In the colours of his hair
(In the woven braids of his hair)
The women whisper secrets from their cave
(The women entice you from the lair)
The tides will rise at 4, don't be late
(The tides rise at 4, please don't be late)

I give him the gift of remembrance as my wish
(I give him the gift of remembrance as my gift)
To give him peace of mind, and a chance to forget
(To give him peace in his mind, and a chance to forget)

Paint his face ashen
(Paint his face ashen)
Draw your face cold
(Draw your face cold)
A man without sorrow
(A man without fire)
Is a man without soul
(Is man without soul)

the restless word

I write the restless word for you
That is no secret
But what I wish to say is hidden from view
Amongst childish strains of laughter
Escaping daylight gravity
I circle round for a better view

Soft skies follow
And green grass calls
But it is hope that pulls me here
I picture myself as independent
Free from the menace and sway that threatens to swallow down
    all that is being begun, delivered anew

I picture you soft and careless
Dropping minutes as you move
And if you arrive open
Will you close the door behind you?
And bring fresh flowers to place beneath my bed
It is as certain as Sunday
Or the scrawl on my walls

Mother Mary herself will place the shawl on your shoulders
And the sea will carry you home
In the warm rush of a wish
I write the restless word for you
That is no secret

lay me down

They lay me down
And gild me with lilies, "please"
And ask me to sleep
To lean towards the drum of my own heart
Familiar and rare this is
Whatever was seeking can be found there, with care
Wrapped in rice paper and folded just so
Whatever was wanting can be sought anew
By breaking the seals and renewing the vows

My hands go up, my head goes back
And the Creator speaks my true name
I am here for healing
I open my body
and in the dream
carefully pull out each one of my vital organs
Placing them on my blanket to heal in the sun
I am grateful to know these visions
Because time is different here

They pick me up and inspect my wounds
To see if I am breathing
And leaving way too soon
Whatever was needed will find its way home
Delivered with riches and prayers full of soul

Now off in my journeys
I forget who I am

The places I've lost in
And the spot where I stand
Whatever was seeking gets a question in return
Because time knows different answers here

cherry blossoms

In the thrall of winter are we
Quietly stirring whatever nightfall sets aside
Cherry blossoms grow silently in our rooms
To build branches for toy birds who cannot sing

Our pace is hurried till gloom shakes us to
To swipe cobwebs from the warm nest
I count every last secret as sleep sneaks in
Figuring how to trade my loose fillings for pretty things

Within the clutch I lead armies to vainglorious victory
Feign courage in the face of titanic struggles
To raise up my brothers and sisters from piles of ash
Securing my place among them

Swiftly dawn rides in bringing threads to pull
To unravel souls that I should find greeting
Outside us the embrace is set to spring
Ready to awaken thirst

the follies of summer

Quicksand, ocean sky
Wondering, don't ask me why or how we got here
We just did
The most eternal sun-drenched kiss is locked in my mind as
    something I won't miss
Or even try to remember
Summer has come and gone so many times I've lost count
Endless, nameless, marked by time as nothing special
But the warmth is here, you see
In darling soliloquy
Hidden in costume and fine-boned prose
Under canopies of sheltered light and life
Summer is here and it is all mine

see saw swam

I saw the cross
The fields
The church where I pray
I withstood the train
Only inches from my body
Screaming down the rails
I swam the quarry
Where nobody ever came
Except to lose everything
I saw the house
The cord they cut him down from
Skipping rope under the sun
I touched the belt
That laid the welts
And dented the refrigerator
I knew the kids
The runts amuck
Running among the bungalow ruts
I tasted snow
The grin
The yellowjacket wings making death rattles
I watched the planes going somewhere close
Chasing 3 sisters thru a wasteland
I was the loneliness
The dead battery
The rockets shot up with no regard to where they would land
I imagined the coast while you slept
And wept from the guilt of the films

That never stop running
I cleaned the stains
And the fists
And the loss of what's real to me

imperial swan

Box a clutter
Junk on the nails
Swan bathes nightly
Kingdoms they fail
Leapfroggin' touch
Whatever they climb
High high higher
Shutting voices flat

Backdoor swing
Check pulse go!
Hot
They blow tops
Into nothing
Pineapple faces
Scratching their arms
Chipping the low waters
For a little harmony

Praying in taxis
Frayed at the end
Give a zip gun
I'll lend you some friends
Eluding everything
The kiss and the gleam
Scraping black seeds
Into your teeth

Film over
Credits die
Sleep thru others
Others they find
Keys click
Heels tick
Fancy odes spilling
Lines missed
Missing out
But getting in
Here's my stop
Call me again

a wax seal

My back is full of insect wings
Collectors poke and scalpels ring
The gospel here according to me
Says I shouldn't be feeling any such thing

Beneath
I stretch out the wait slow
To keep safe my keepsakes
Till I build up enough steam to run out of steam to float upstream
    to lands of forgotten kings

To a church riddle I throw this
Who belongs and who goes
I ride with my twin however I pose
And we just go
We just go
Off to the others, by cover, by night
Atop the lights and rooftops bright

My cavity fills up with sea-sick word
Disabled ably often to catch the first bird
I wrap such chaos sweet with bow
And send it off on the backs of a hundred crows
Tied with white ribbons

Alright, I'll get to the point
I'm lost without and kept within

I never wanted this thought to take hold
Cause beginnings with you seem different
Apologies if I tripped that wire
The one attached to desire

collapse

What becomes of the passage
The stealing away at dawn
And the coarse tongue
Thirsting for love

What becomes of the phantoms
And their midnight parades
Will we still risk the signal
Whistling in your latest and greatest endeavours

And what becomes silence
And the darkness that follows
Who will take hold of whatever is still left
From here to there

Where goes the laughter
And all the hidden coil
Who shall tend to the hand-built bridges
That sheltered us rising

Where goes the wander
And the fine coats stitched
Who finds the trails that lead
To new visions frayed

And who are these angels
You casually invoked
What of their merry makes belief
If our bellow is only for ourselves

Who now lies sleeping
Who dare you single out
To collapse at our village gate
A victim of results

What becomes of the sacred oaths
And the blossoms felled
And the dizzy games
That find us farther than we are

Who shall bring spirits
Who claims chance as their friend
And what of this moment leaves you closer
To leave me again

a most cautious wit

Oh sob and spit, cautious wit!
Get lost in this
Devotion to oblivion lends strength to chatterboxes that take coins
    from empty pockets
I know your visions forsaken
And the abyss where kisses drain
For it delivers as it should
Such arrows are fire for you to sling
From ear to ear and ring to ring
My colours mix most everything
Get lost in this
Get lost in this.

Travelers knock, you let them in
To mock your silence and quiet worn thin
As your judge I justly rule
You're guilty of madness and boors, all fools
They deliver to me your very sting
To leave flat and be neatly tucked away
When the moon opaque sits on your belly
I shift your focus to eclipse
Place your hand on my heart and your wish on my hips
Sit still, my friend, occasional confidante
Let's get lost in this, lost in this.

simple riddle rhymes

simple riddle rhymes
insinuations of heartaches yet to be overrun
by conquering finches flinching their way across no-man's-land
a war of nerves
of nervous stomachs and elixir cures
mixed just right with mercury and western longing

an aging apostle cuts into caricature
could he possibly envision the cowboy hats and dusty boots
caked with Indian blood and vampire bats' blood
blood that will one day come to settle old scores
as we move the hills bounce back their echo fade
and the whiff of their ephemeral remains

digging trenches deep
we loosed our grip on childish sleep
we were laid bare to behold what we'd one day reap
and keep
tied in tearstained handkerchiefs
stuffed in breast pockets, closer to heart's hold
riding high in wagon wheel ruts
the roosters strut
and the lonesome wail

a voice rides up
recognized as the familiar voice of our own yearnings
what is it that we want so bad?
If life is attached to vague purpose
Must our deaths be heroic as well?

How does this play to the constituencies of the flatlands and cities
    alike?

My apostle, he ran scared
His cross tossed eagerly into a ditch
My god failing up above
And me failing down below
It helps to have a good name to cling to at a time like this
My name was Emma Lee
Not mine, but hers
That's who I held on to while I cursed the sun

a portrait of oblivion

I paint this portrait of oblivion
To amuse and diffuse mine enemy
To incite anarchy in thy heart

There is no nature under Mother Earth
That is not met in mortal decay
Only the mutual dance of stale air and agreed-upon motions
    escapes her glance

True genius is a virus that must invade and destroy their construct
    connections
Alas, I call to arms all the saints and archangels too
To dislodge the mask of howling aspiration

Her mystery seeks to reel me, to strip me of power
To wrap me in snakebites
To call down upon me her sister asps
I have a stake in all things pure
Mine is the shudder of the malnourished
And the bleating song of kiddie tears
Together they are weakness
I alone dislodge their heavy mask of sanctity

Her blood on me is communion
In mercury water and the moon crisp, shock gathered
No boundaries exist between nations
Only forest and desert plain awake with rape and horror
It is the dark that draws us deeper
Her secrets that slice us open to our own sound and shame

A spectacle of self is jarred loose from raw bone
We're left to engage all comers
And late bloomers and rooty-tooters
And the sons of soothsayers
In slick dialogues on heaven and hells
That are sweet to the eyes and ear
But nails in the stomach

Let me remind you of genius
The wash of healers and robed mystics
Bedeviled and jeweled in a forever crown
The stars will line up for me

all roads

Gather me up some stars
Sprinkled from your eyes
Beckon forth the little sighs

Should all roads disappear but one
Then leave while I am sleeping

These hours watching from windows
Play music without autumn
The scripting of light
Moves ever so slight
Wherever I sit today

Hands go thru glass
And dreams thru you
Whatever passes as chance
Also passes for truth

May I tumble
May I call
May I find you at all

armadillo

armadillo trains rustle underfoot
cool deserts jangle in spirits
we ride the night across this empty husk
I am your eternal love

Can't you see my reflection in your window?
Mixed soft with neon candy glow
and teenage sonic boom
In nights spent creeping thru your room
All these thoughts end way too soon

Their bones are out there still
Baking in the sun and lunar ocean light alike
To be found one day like us
As stories we cannot bear to listen to

siam mais

I am free
To give my heart freely
With no string attached
To roam, to hurt
To be devastated as I so wish
To be ravished by freedom
My youth
So bound do I knock against her cages
If she holds lock and key

I am free
To give you my heart
This notion suits me, bears weight
What is false and old is not ours to hold
We have never owned or possessed anything true in our whole
    lives, except maybe each other

I see myself in you and that is a dangerous thing
But is this friendship alive?
Does it breathe when no one is listening?
Does it know when I am sleeping?

Stories can be retold
Until they are polished smooth
I give my heart to you in this story
Because my heart has no end

wants of some desires

I'm given to wants of some desires
And given to wants of none at all
For fires consumed burn ever so bright
Unable to be drenched in the place of my soul

From a drowsy spot just on the other side of sleep
Did you dream well, as I did of another
And another time altogether?
Lay such hand upon my brow
And take me with you as you leave

For some light must penetrate old shadows
And I want you with sword in hand
To cross left over right, dark over night
You over me, me under you

A confessor once spoke kind
That he loved all that he abhorred
For it kept him fixed in a place beyond nature
But things do shift, and that same confessor
Confesses to you
That my love,
As it once loved
Loves no more

the princess of apples

Princess, I've seen you
So lost now for so long
Simple grace is my touch in it
Because I gave up somewhere
A face I've forgotten now

And like you, I spoiled the whispers
And cut as my own ghosts of shale
The water still runs down these walls
Where we made vows of time
They put their mark here and so shall we
In epitaphs and minor regrets

So we are lost now for too long
Too long to remember how
Too close to shake the tree
For silver apples and baby bees

a bunch of words

Curses lick lips locked browbeaten hills touch sallow codes decipher
glyphs gleaming darkness leaps spines shallow Clementine kisses
asphyxiating needs needy thrills thrill dial toning spaces link rivers
run mountains mount misery cutting cords stripped raw useless
coughing tangents delivered sights seeking people movers spurs
silver sidewinders coiled boiling ready steady no groove able willing
enable fire at will spilling guts under caress dresses beauty regrets
confessions mistakes misshapen omitting transmissions sets weary
carnival remembrances riding tonight high paper kites aw shucks
fuck misstep north eyes realize exposed endings nails wishing envy
window hope aperture drawing dawn killing cards babies blinking
enough already hands dancing shoes shady lanes calliope caterwaul
inhaling hail chaos failing possession tumbling obelisk airtight
ceiling arise smokestack lightning

bedroom jungle

Wading chest high in the Mississippi mud
Slipping downstream slow as you please
Lovers stroll for gentle shade
Flies buzz buzz
my father pushes hair off my face
We are all in the frame together

Lying knee deep in a pissed-up bed
Monsters crawling on the ceiling
And I'm wishing death
Is Jack London really from London?
The call of the wild is the rain on my face
20 bucks in my pocket says I can make it to Alaska

the dogs will wail along the Ganges
as the river rolls by
my body burns goodbyes
like so many discarded prayers

the song of the earth

I live in memory
But I am not any such thing that you can touch as a pleasure, or
    lust for spring
Sing the song of the earth and know everything

I am a lazy river forgotten within you
But I am not any such thing you can deny
Sing the song of the earth and you must cry from the waves lapping
    at your door

We all fawn overreaching beyond humble goals
Thinking that by trying or dying we needn't finish what we started
Sing the song of the earth and millions die
Telling stories backwards

We rumble our feet to no response
Cut down every tree to count the rings
Hollow to the core her supple body
And demand the void come before us
Sing the song of the earth and know the secret is no seeker after all

We sing the song of the earth as we rest
As the old scenes are worn down with rain
Children are allowed to forget
So we live as memory and they live tomorrow

The song of the earth is never done
So sing it as it must be sung
Into my ear she'll listen
Confessing all

disciples

Radiate disciples

Radiate

Where we touch is unseen

Violet embrace

All manner of the chrysalis signals

The code of the Christ

It's as if I am inside you

I understand so much of what you need

But so little of what you ask

Allow this moment to pass us by

Stand by my side

Radiate thru me

Within tombs destined

They honor devotion

To a cause that isolates us from a path of freedom

Such tears well inside me of pride and lament

Radiate little bird

You are heaven sent to me

the box

inside this box I put
my mother's things
false teeth
2 wedding rings
pictures of beautiful youth
her worn-out couch and window gaze
a razor voice like mine
2 kitty cats named Trouble and Harmony
75 clocks running backwards
some collector's plates of Oz
but there isn't any music

zen poem

life/the flickering candle
life/thick van gogh paint
life/the patient answer
life is the greatest thing

thought/the open flower
thought/the humming scream
thought/the traffic light
thought is communion

love/eternal circles
love/the spinning child
love/the playful servant
love is quicksand

feelings/the great protector
feelings/the vengeful wasp
feelings/the paint peeling
feelings are our reminder

life/the dying tornado
life/the blistering peal
life/the aging icon
life is a victory lap

thought/the winter solstice
thought/the history book
thought/the river secrets
thought the messenger boy

love/the hushed churches
love/the forgotten joke
love/the quiet asylum
love is just double dare

feelings are coney island
feelings/the fingered crook
feelings/the lost traveler
feelings are like spilling milk

death

Floating, I am caressed in details
So that I might forget might and right
Cracked in the marrow for the morrow of youthful plunder has no
    place here
not now

I am breath
Wasting into teacups
Signaling leave so I run forever
That I may love you to the end of my days

What is love without loss
and is but lost without love?

are jewels beneath the sea
dropped from your hand like so many forgotten petitions
luminating this vigil within
the wait, an elemental ploy few desire
but so many chase

a rose i suppose

What's to look for?
A rose I suppose
Buttercups and honeycombs
Pearl-handled brushes and love-letter poems
Some chattering prose on copper wire
Climbing up an ivory tower

What's to look for?
Any rose I suppose
Suppose they all smell good
And cover the stench of death
Any rose will do
Just throw them lightly on my lapis lazuli inlaid tomb
It's so simple I could cry
This need I have to connect with you

What's to seek?
A new rose I suppose
Fire red with petals of dread
So much trouble I just had to try
Didn't I?

This rose, this rose was mine
And now I'm on about a rose
Your rose I suppose
But I threw you out my window
To the cold gray below
And the riverbed of a bright, sunny morning.

taos

tearing open the bramble brush and speakeasy earth
land ho!!
"America is my place"
a place to ponder and plunder

fishing rocks out of the river
putting them in his pocket to take home
to be set on his mantelpiece to dial in the old energies
to make a clear way
"America is my way"

end times found at the ends of trails
where hissing dogs guard gates
broken open from neglect
what do they protect if not the past?

lighting burnt sage
asking his grandparents what to do
"when silence is left here for the ages coming?"

fumbling with rusted keys and Tahitian locks
he sought his people, my people
"what happened here?"
bodies cover in shame
faces drop
fleeing to sit on hindquarters and watch from the low hills
"come back," he said speaking,
"I used to drink from these same rivers as a child"

then he could not wait to leave
to go out seeking from the quiet
so that he should know what is

seeking land to hide
erecting a temple there for himself
stone by stone, tile by tile
until it shone of sacrifice
dedicating it to Juno
consecrating their union in madness
sleeping on her floor
writing his verse by cold light
to possess her fully
held alive in the living things
and her devotions to the unseen
seasons passed, his anger grew ripe
in his contract and birthright
he seeded the void

in forever
she parts her hair down the center
making pretty braids and pretty threats
never allowing him to forget times passed up easy
to find promises today
he read her what he had written
until he was more than before

courage

There is of course the courage of a single flower
Pushing its form thru concrete
If only to be trampled into dust

What is worth speaking
If seeking is death?
Does meaning become
Meaningless?

Summoning up the voice
To do the will of the soul
To explore the far reaches of my wonder
I make the choice to speak

Is it so simple
That it's easy to overlook
That living is poetry
And poetry nothing less

years of grace

little survives what time has passed by
my years of grace mistaken for lost wanderings
no more alive than a remembrance stained in your sufferings
my years of grace deliver proud

at last rest stumbles, so pull your covers tight
to whom do I speak thru echoes threadbare
what survives the rush of the profane
and their words mere dust one swallows to believe

true poets dare listen to the stars dead and cold
I sold you out for moonbeams dying to shine
Illuminated by what has survived
and years of grace to come

marigold

I look up and the rain is tap-tap-tapping in
Strong and cold, it beats out ancient rhythms of loneliness
My people were here so long ago
Did they cry and die like I am?
Or did a simpler time bring a simpler heart?
I can't imagine their echo died any different in those days, on these
    walls
Found as chaste desires that hung on the moon and her tides alone

The trickster rides his horse laughing
He says, "you fool, you fool . . .
You can't bring love anywhere you are not patient . . .
Love will not sit waiting!"
Well throw me a rope trickster
Let me climb out and up into the light
To kiss the sky with dirty fingers
And wail for my father's father
And ask the spirits "where did everyone go?"

At the bottom of my hole lies a soul so cold
Collecting aqua blue marigold
If you are willing to dive for love this deep
You might find all that you seek

solace

Seeking peace and solace on a Sunday morning
Long walk, all children smile hello
There's so much laughter to soak by fingertip
But strangers are dangerous
Even kids know that
A lily pond to quench my thirst
All manner of words destroyed by rippling water
I don't run, I walk, say the gods
A poke into reflection
A moment's chance to make good
Forget it, I say
This loneliness is easy to bear
Nature laughs it, so I become

dares for dreamtime

I have the marks of a child reborn
400 blessings as forgiveness
Fears cascading down to my feet
In the haunted times I have counted the blows taken
Foreshadowing claims of misery as my own child
To caress yet never smile upon

Let the rivers run thru me like spoilt milk
I will caress you in dreamtime with soft hands
Tear scars from the flesh
And beg you to speak resonant bells

Her image fused belief
The courage to trust a thief
If only for a moment
This is tribute to me
I am grateful and petulant and I do not want to know what cannot
be persuaded

On old boats lazy we drift
Unwashed in the morning sun
Cold and shivering
Can you feel what I ask?
Touch your nose, eyes closed
The dream reappears
Only to disappear just like that!

clutching breath

The whispers are mine
And the bellyaches
And the leaves that turn yellow with cheerless succor?
Mine, all mine

There are stories I told you that I hold from escaping
To clutch your breath at the nape of your sweet failings
Falling up into clutches
Calling the secret names embedded in your thirst
So that I may drink to you, to forget

The dirt of too many gangways has soiled my suits
I hate to even look at them as they writhe
But walk on them I did
Like my brothers who hide their sad poems inside their sisters

the river runs foul

The river runs foul
from the gates where my father once stood
down to the apple trees
from mirror to the gutter
we run streaks of stardust
and funny dumb dreams of shattered warmth
happiness is nothing but a smile

I detect her here in the warm night air
I move silent, I do not wish to be seen

The river runs south
Thru ghettos and starched neighborhood squares
And everywhere the dogs howl
I don't even trust the hum of my own voice here
My own impermanence haunts me
But this thought alone relieves the pressure
From the mirrors to the gutters done
Gutter tongued, my heart speaks to the silence in me
Let me walk alone, home
As the dead stoplights wave good night

for the warmth of the morning

Straining for the warmth of the morning
I need to be filled with hope
If you sent me a flower each and every day
I would be fulfilled
(I would feel fulfilled)
Never to leave, never to roam

The water brings the day in slow sweep
Only to bring us back to these desires
I am the rhythm if I walk alone
(I stole the rhythm of you alone)
Where I rise I ask myself where you are
I'm so tired of that question
There should be a presence
A presence between us

I know you were born with a carnival spirit
There is no taming such a tiger or thing like that
You've got the streets to possess you
Royalty surrounded by such confusion that there is no peace
    to bring
Only the drums of happenstance and revelry will do
My God, you carve out my heart so
I am not from your boulevards, but dark attics
Can you see that now?
You broke the news to me that I was a poet
I'd love to swear I was cheap with words but I know it's not true
For you it's sonnets and bonnets and tales of Rasputin
Could I ever trust a creature so blue?

For you belong to the earth now
So finely so
I bought you the alley cats and the rags torn
All for you to dot your eyes and cross your feet
You are within me so this is all

the passions

Sun blanches the soul
Searching for seashells along the seashore
The passions are lost with age, yet sweet
beneath a glance
Time washing out the colors of my coat
To horizon points north, to roam
"how far?" goes the chorus
"how far do we have to go?" goes me
I think I'd rather not care to know
No matter the presentation
To see is sorrow
And sorrow sees much more than I

This morn I will write you letters sealed in tears
With drawing of cages and animals extinct
Mailed from the farthest parts of here
Where my remains hope unashamed
and storms collide just beneath the eyes

this heartache

This heartache spoils that which is willing and good and so true
I've measured each and every step to protect the one thought I hold
   dear
Oh, wretched, wretched you!
Cursed, cursed you!

Why remain a ghost when faith is only vapor?
To scorn all that would obstruct your path?
A path chosen by you for you alone
A soul as I has no place to go, only to roam
Thru Roman streets fought for by thee
To sit under cedars to watch the poppies cut slow
To have and to hold
To love and let go

There is no heartache for that which isn't true
This heartache spoils that which is willing you away

pussywillows

Pussywillows, in amongst
Twisting your fingers
Too much rope to mend
Bending a dream or two or three
A delight
And should I become approximately last
I will not hesitate to fall and forgetfully flee
Demanding, these pussywillow things
Because they never die

Lingering on as devious draws upon a well-worn psyche
Fraught with flaws and aching jaws
Not in the least forgetting the tired paeans to discerning muses
Amused by ruses to feign sleep while slipping off the knot
How I have missed your meanings ever so bright?

My slate bed being cold on eves of despair
Makes me think merrily of your cheer
A free state follows of course, of any enamoring pull
And arrives faithfully to be given away by invitation only
Under weeping willow you
And I, beholden to Pan and sway of the sight
Of pussywillows, delight

gingerbread

Cautions for you gingerbread
From the ones who stand in line
Asking for secrets and any spare junk you might have
Left by the door

Count me in however you choose
The Irish don't have much left to lose but
Sanities that deprive and vanities that prevail
If you wind my clocks, you'll climb my walls
I give it all away, and then some more
I pull out what's left by its tendrils
But there's always another piece
It's boring, but I can't figure out another trick

To set the boundaries up tight
I'd like to curl up behind you
In the wheel well
Listen to the motor purr
And wonder where we are headed next
Thru streets that nip and tuck to the nether hours
It took me a year to arrive, but here I am
Set on listening, but mostly forgetting

in the eyes beholding

in the eyes beholding
her aspects of arcane pleasure
slaving in such magnet measures
to repel and attract

I am your bones shattered
I am the breath seeking
I am such senses creaking
'neath chandeliers of night

flat pools of warm surrender
cruel summer of aging truth
my search was never ending
until I sought you

think not of virgin terrors
think not of family claim
wipe clean the dying embers
with my name

ease thru darkened hallways
ascend to highest high
call your deceivers down to you
drown them in their knives

cause we are the eyes beholding
let them spell our watch
let them try to divide us
for we are already conquered

painting shade

There are but 10,000 dreams
I'd put them all in my hand if you'd let me
But that would be too easy
And I'm too graceful a gazelle to be seen drifting
So together we can make hard work of the good life
To know just how good life really is

Here the piñons die thirsty
And the arsenic boils in my blood
As I jump off the bridge with angel arms
This is a message waiting for you
And the message will never change
Your ancestors, when hollowed out by their hungers
Climbed over oceans to get here
They figured you might need to know someday
That nothing changes but the rules of man against God's law

Put away your gun gringo
Lasso somebody else's heart
Let a cowboy be a cowpoke with boyish charm
So you can paint shade with your hands
Don't fight what's yours
Don't steal what's theirs
And don't listen too hard
To who's coming up the stairs

the poetry of oblivion

I wake
Scan the horizon for your heartbeat
Are you still there?
Tired is not a word
Words like weariness come to mind
Devastation as a place in time

So it's all dramatic, no pause necessary
This place moves at the same speed wherever you are
Which is way too fast
This is supposed to be the poetry of oblivion
Towers toppling and gatekeepers crashing
But I've become plain and awful
Awful strange, awful funny, awfully, woefully, awe-full
An eyesore upon ragged earth and barren soil
Shoeless wandering upon her scars

I sit in this spot, Ben Franklin of all people looking on
Chicago hasn't got its heroes straight
Just on the other side of the road is a statue of Hans Christian
    Andersen
Maybe these men were important here before Chicago got its
    own heroes
Like Al Capone, bang bang!
Or Ernie Banks, hey hey!

It all started right and ended wrong
"I miss you" went his poetry of oblivion
lost in so many words

I found this lyric torn
"blacktop fingertips . . .
black cat wail . . .
full moon's hiding . . .
when hell is on my tail . . ."
my bed is empty without your pretty face
the poetry of my sorrow is written in these words

i choose

I choose
to invoke my right
of myth
Upon
the drawstrings
of the phantom
mother
Just above
Come to gift the past

creatures

Exotic creatures
Tear me up
You have lives and problems due
My belonging
Strong in essence
Is but torn under light
I squander fortunes on your comfort
But you leave me behind
to figure in figures
and coil my fingers fine
so deliver me this last
aligned we can win
they'll sweep the floors with their hair
and I can have innocence
and make believe
it's fine, this time we have had

Printed in the USA
CPSIA information can be obtained
at www.ICGtesting.com
LVHW091147150724
785511LV00005B/604

9 780571 211708